SMART SCIENCE

Force

Robert Snedden

Heinemann Library
Des Plaines, Illinois

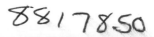

Text designed by Visual Image
Cover designed by M2
Illustrations by Paul Bale, Peter Bull and Jane Watkins
Printed in Hong Kong

03 02 01 00 99
10 9 8 7 6 5 4 3 2 1

Library of Congress Cataloging-in-Publication Data

Snedden, Robert.
    Forces / Robert Snedden.
        p. cm. -- (Smart science)
    Includes bibliographical references and index.
    Summary: Discusses various aspects of forces, including gravity, magnetism, Newton's laws, inertia, friction, action and reaction, velocity, acceleration, balanced forces, combined forces, elastic energy, and more.
    ISBN 1-57572-869-9 (lib. bdg.)
    1. Force and energy—Juvenile literature. 2. Force and energy——Study and teaching (Elementary)—Activity programs—Juvenile literature. [1. Force and energy.] I. Title. II. Series.
    QC73.4.S64   1999
    531'.6—dc21   98-49853
                                                              CIP
                                                              AC

Acknowledgments
The publisher would like to thank the following for permission to reproduce photographs:
Action-Plus/Steve Bardens, p. 6; Peter Tarry, p. 12; Glyn Kirk, p. 17; J. Allan Cash, pp. 5, 8, 13; Empics/Matthew Ashton, p. 7; Michael Steele, p. 10; Tony Marshall, p. 24; FLPA/E & D Hosking, p. 29; Sally & Richard Greenhill, p.28; Robert Harding Picture Library, p. 15; Trevor J. Hill, p. 14; Explorer/JP Lescourret, p. 4; Brian Hawkes, p. 9; Photri/Tom Sanders, p. 11; Military Picture Library, p. 27; Peter Russell, p. 18; Science Photo Library/Prof. Harold Edgerton, p. 16; Takeshi Takahara, p. 19; NASA, pp. 20, 21; Adam Hart-Davis, p. 25; Simon Fraser, p. 26.

Cover photograph reproduced with permission of Allsport (Vincent LaForet)

Every effort has been made to contact copyright holders of any material reproduced in this book. Any omissions will be rectified in subsequent printings if notice is given to the Publisher.

Note to the Reader
Some words in this book are shown in bold, **like this.** You can find out what they mean by looking in the glossary.

CONTENTS

FORCES IN ACTION

Forces push and forces pull. Forces make things move, and forces stop things that were moving. Forces can make moving objects speed up, slow down, and change direction. Forces press things together, and forces pull things apart. Forces are at work whenever and wherever **energy** is being used.

Children in a playground exert a number of pushing and pulling forces.

Feel the Force

When you stand up, you push back on your chair to move yourself up. With every step you take, you push against the ground. When you breathe deeply, the muscles in your chest force your chest to expand. When you turn the pages of this book, you exert a force that pulls the pages up and over. And all the time, there are also forces acting on you.

Universal Forces

Forces can act on scales that are both unimaginably big and invisibly small. Powerful forces hold together **atoms**, the tiny particles that make up all of the materials around us. The force of **gravity** keeps the earth traveling around the sun.

The force of gravity may be one of the weakest forces, but it acts across the entire universe.

Closer to home, gravity pulls you back down to the ground when you jump up. A force is something that acts on an object. All objects, no matter how big or how small, have forces acting on them. Forces are acting on us all of the time.

Action at a Distance

Some forces are only felt when one object touches another. When you kick a ball, you impart a force that changes its speed and direction. If you miss the ball, it does not move. Kicking is a contact force. Other forces, such as gravity and **magnetism**, are non-contact forces. They can make an object move without actually touching it.

It's a Fact— Nuclear Force

The strongest of all forces work over the shortest of distances. These are the nuclear forces that hold together the tiny atoms from which all materials are made.

Try This—Force of Attraction

You need: wool clothes, a balloon, and a helper

What to do: Rub the balloon against some wool and then hold it above your helper's head. Watch as your helper's hair is attracted to the balloon. This is caused by an **electrostatic** force, which you produced by rubbing the balloon against the wool. Like gravity and magnetism, electrostatic forces can act at a distance.

FORCES IN MOTION

Objects are in motion everywhere you look. Aircraft fly overhead, people walk and run, and trees sway in the wind. On a grander scale, the earth travels around the sun, taking you through the year.

Newton's Laws

Whether it is the earth's movement around the sun, or the flight of a ball from your hand as you throw it, motion can be described by three simple scientific **laws**. These laws of motion were discovered by Sir Isaac Newton.

Newton's first law says that an object will stay still or, if moving, continue to move at the same speed and in the same direction, unless it is acted on by a force. All objects tend to keep moving at the same speed and in the same direction. This is called **inertia**. Once an object is moving, it will move forever unless other forces act on it. On Earth, the forces of **friction** and **gravity** stop this from happening.

The baseball pitcher exerts a force that sets the ball in motion.

The batter will exert a force and try to change the ball's direction.

A Change of Direction

Newton's second law says that a force acting on an object will cause the object to move in the direction of the force. How far and how fast the object moves depends on the size of the object and the size of the force. If you hit a ball to the left, you would not expect it to suddenly go right. Nor would you expect to be able to hit the ball very far if it were made of solid, heavy rock.

It's a Fact—Sir Isaac Newton

Many people believe Isaac Newton (1643–1727)was the greatest scientist who ever lived. Along with his work on motion and gravity, he investigated light and invented a new system of mathematics called calculus. The unit of force—the newton—was named after him.

Try This—Marbles in Motion

You need: marbles of different sizes, a flat surface, and a helper

What to do: Roll a marble along the surface and ask your friend to roll another toward it so that they collide. When they collide, the marbles exert a force on each other. Watch carefully to see which directions the marbles go. What happens when one marble is bigger than the other? Try side and head-on collisions to see what happens.

Action and Reaction

Newton's third law says that for every action, there is an equal but opposite reaction. If you blow up a balloon and let it go, it shoots across the room. The action of the air blowing backwards out of the balloon produces the reaction that pushes the balloon forward. Whenever you push or pull an object, it pushes or pulls you with equal force.

Jet Propulsion

A jet engine also works according to Newton's third law. A powerful fan sucks air into the engine. The air is heated inside a combustion chamber, where fuel is burned. The heated air expands very rapidly and rushes from the back of the engine. This creates a reaction force, or **thrust**, on the engine that makes the aircraft fly forward.

Jet engines demonstrate action and reaction, producing a forward thrust by expelling hot gases backwards out of the engine exhausts.

Stopping a Moving Object

A moving object possesses **energy** of motion, called **kinetic energy**. Just how much energy it has depends on how heavy the object is and how fast it is traveling. In physics, **momentum** (M) is defined as the **mass** (m) of the object multiplied by its **velocity** (v), or M=mv. The momentum of an object changes only when it is acted upon by an outside force. A skillful fielder catching a fast-moving ball exerts sufficient force to stop it. The momentum of the ball is transferred to the catcher's hands, pushing them back as the ball is caught. The greater the momentum, the greater the force needed to stop the object.

A locomotive, which weighs several tons, has a great deal of momentum because of its huge mass, even when traveling very slowly.

It's a Fact—Magnetic Reaction

Newton's third law also applies to **magnetism**. If a piece of iron is attracted to a magnet, the magnet is also attracted to the iron, with an equal and opposite force.

Try This—Balloon Racers

You need: balloons, lengths of cotton, drinking straws, thumbtacks, and sscotch tape

What to do: Cut lengths of thread long enough to stretch from wall to wall across a room. Fasten one end of the thread to a wall using a thumbtack. Then pass the thread through a drinking straw and fasten the other end of the thread to the opposite wall. Blow up your racing balloon. Then, keeping the neck pinched closed, tape the balloon to the straw. Let the balloon go and watch as action and reaction sends it flying!

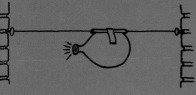

VELOCITY AND ACCELERATION

The speed at which an object is traveling is a measure of the distance it moves in a certain amount of time. If you cycle at a speed of 10 mph (16 km/h), you will travel 5 miles (8 kilometers) in 30 minutes. Scientists talk about **velocity** rather than speed. Velocity takes into account not only of how fast an object is traveling, but also the direction it is traveling in.

Going Faster

If a force continues to push or pull an object, its speed will steadily increase. This increase in speed is called **acceleration**. A car picking up speed as it drives away from a traffic light is accelerating as its engine pulls it along. A skydiver hurtling towards the ground is accelerating as the force of **gravity** pulls him or her faster and faster toward the ground.

The effort this cyclist is putting into increasing his speed is obvious.

The faster the speed increases, the greater the acceleration. Acceleration measures how fast speed is gained. In other words, acceleration is how many more feet per second faster you go with every second that passes.

Terminal Velocity

Earth's gravity accelerates a falling object, whether it is a skydiver or a dropped glass, at a rate of nearly 33 feet (10 meters) per second per second. This means that after 10 seconds, the object would be traveling at 300 feet (100 meters) per second or 225 mph (360 km/h). Of course, gravity is not the only force acting on a falling object. The faster an object falls through the air, the more the air resists it. The force of gravity and the air resistance balance each other out, and the object stops accelerating. When this happens, the object has reached its final speed, or **terminal velocity**. Terminal velocity depends on how much air resistance an object has. For a skydiver, it is around 118 mph (190 km/h).

It's a Fact—Light Speed

Light travels through space at around 186,000 mi/sec (300,000 km/sec).

Try This—Swing Time

You need: a swing

What to do: Sit on the swing and start swinging! As you move the swing forward and backward, you are speeding up and slowing down all the time. You push yourself up, and gravity pulls you back down. You accelerate as you push up. Gravity slows you down and then accelerates you back toward the ground again, and so on.

FORCES IN BALANCE

Why do some things stand still? That might seem to be a silly question at first, but all objects have forces acting on them all the time. If something stays still, it is because the forces acting on it are in balance.

Balanced Forces

Imagine a tug-of-war between two equally strong teams. Both teams pull as hard as they can, but nothing happens. The forces they are exerting on the rope are in balance. They are pulling with equal force, but in opposite directions, and so the two forces cancel each other out. Even when you are sitting still on a chair, there are forces in balance. The force of your weight presses down on the chair, but the chair does not collapse because it meets this downward force with an equal and opposite upward force.

Sumo wrestlers are temporarily balanced as each tries to exert more force than the other.

Buildings and Bridges

When architects and engineers design buildings and bridges, they pay close attention to the forces that will be acting on the structures. The forces have to be in balance or else the structures could collapse.

The complex structure of the Forth Railway Bridge in England is carefully designed to balance the load it carries.

A bridge has to be able to support the weight of the traffic that travels over it. The piers at each end of a simple bridge and the cables supporting a suspension bridge provide the upwards force, or upthrust, to balance the weight of traffic on the bridge. A building has to be able to support the weight of its roof and everything the building contains.

It's a Fact—How Helicopters Hover

A helicopter hovers because the uplift force of its rotors exactly balances the downward pull of **gravity**.

Try This—Building Bridges

You need: two chairs of the same height, sheets of stiff cardboard, and weights

What to do: Position the chairs about a yard apart. Place a piece of cardboard on each chair so that half of it juts out into the gap between the chairs. Put a weight (a couple of heavy books) on top of each piece of cardboard to hold it in place. Put a third piece of cardboard over the first two to complete the bridge. How much weight can you put in the middle of the bridge before it collapses? Try increasing the weights on the chairs. Does this make a difference? The downward force of the weights produces an equal and opposite upthrust that supports the two sides of the bridge. How strong is your bridge without the weights?

COMBINED FORCES

It is not unusual for an object to be acted upon by more than one force at the same time. These forces add together to produce an effect on the object. This combination of forces is called the **resultant** force.

Resultant Forces

When you throw a ball, it follows a curved path through the air because there are two forces acting on it. First, there is the force you gave to it by throwing it. This sends it forward through the air at a constant speed. Second, there is the force of **gravity** pulling it down toward the ground. The resultant force is a combination of the two.

Two people can combine lifting forces to move heavier objects than either person could move alone.

If the forces are equal and acting in opposite directions, they will cancel each other out, and the resultant force will be zero. The forces are balanced, and the object does not move. Every time you pick something up, you are producing an unbalanced force. You have to exert an upward force that is stronger than the downward force produced by the weight of the object you are lifting.

It's a Fact—Strictly for Birds

A bird flying through the air causes air to flow over its wings by moving them forward. This creates a **lift**. Lift keeps the bird in the air, just as it does an airplane.

Flying Forces

When an aircraft flies through the air, there are four different forces that need to be considered. First, there is the **thrust** provided by the engines sending the aircraft forward. Second, there is an upward force, called lift, that pushes the wings upward and keeps the aircraft flying. Third, there is air resistance, a frictional force called **drag** that slows the aircraft down as it pushes through the air. Finally, there is the force of gravity pulling the aircraft down toward the ground.

The thrust of an aircraft's engines propel it forward and create lift as the air moves across its wings.

Try This—Which Way Are We Going?

You need: a wheeled cart, two ropes, and a friend

What to do: Attach the ropes to the cart. With your friend, pull it along. You should both try to pull with the same force. See what difference it makes when you both pull straight ahead and then in different directions. You and your friend are exerting two pulling forces on the cart. What is the resultant force?

Squashing and Stretching

Sometimes a force acts on an object that is not able to move. This may make the object change shape. The ability of an object or material to return to its original size and shape after being pushed or pulled by an outside force is called **elasticity**.

It's a Fact— Tennis Anyone?

When a tennis ball strikes a racket at a high speed, the ball is squashed nearly flat by the impact. The ball's **momentum** is absorbed by the elasticity of the ball and the racket strings. The ball's momentum is then rapidly returned as the ball springs back into shape, speeding away from the racket again.

Elastic Materials

When you pull a rubber band, it stretches. You are exerting a force on it. As soon as you let it go, it springs back to its original shape. A rubber band is a good example of an elastic material. Some materials are more elastic than others. Rubber is very elastic, and concrete is not at all elastic.

Elastic Energy

When you **compress** or stretch a spring, you are doing work. As you do so, you are transferring **energy** into the spring. The energy you are storing there is called **elastic potential energy**. As soon as the spring can return to its original shape, this energy will be released.

A pole vaulter is helped over the bar as the pole's elasticity springs it back into shape.

Elastic materials undergo **stresses** and **strains** when acted on by a force. The stress on an object is measured by the strength of the force acting on it. The strain is the amount by which the material changes shape. The higher the stress, the greater the strain.

Elastic Limit

No matter how stretchy a material is, nothing can be stretched forever. Eventually, the material will either snap or just not return to its original shape. When this happens, the material is said to have passed its **elastic limit**.

Try This—Elastic Racers

You need: model cars, strong rubber bands, a long flat board, and thumbtacks

What to do: Anchor the rubber bands at one end of the board using the thumbtacks. Stretch a band back by pulling a car against it. As the band stretches, it is storing the force you are exerting on it. Let the band go. Energy is released as the band springs back to its original shape, propelling the car down the board. Experiment with different thicknesses and greater stretchings of the bands to see how far you can make your cars go.

FRICTION

Why is it easier to pull a heavy object along the ground if it is on wheels? When two things rub together, there is a force called **friction**. It slows things down and stops things that were moving. Friction occurs wherever a moving object comes into contact with another object. Putting wheels on something cuts down on the area of the object that is in contact with the ground. This reduces the friction.

A jet fighter uses a drogue chute to slow its speed by using air resistance and to reduce its landing distance.

Shapes and Surfaces

The amount of friction created is determined by the shape and surface of an object. A ball or wheel rolls freely because of its shape. Only a small part of the ball's surface is in contact with the ground at any one moment. An object of exactly the same weight and material, but shaped like a block, has a lot more of its surface in contact with the ground. It will not move along the ground very easily because there is more friction.

All objects produce friction because nothing is perfectly smooth. Friction can be reduced by lubricating surfaces with oil or grease. Oil is added to car engine parts to reduce the amount of friction between moving parts. Otherwise, the parts would soon wear out.

It is important to keep friction in a car to a minimum. Both its engine parts and its movement along the road create friction.

Air Resistance

An object moving through the air collides with the tiny particles that make up the air. This causes friction. The faster the object is moving, the more collisions there are and the greater the friction. This friction is called air resistance.

It's a Fact—The Heat is On

When you rub your hands together, the heat you feel is caused by friction. When an object is slowed by the friction, it loses some of its **energy** of motion, or **kinetic energy**. Some of this energy is changed into heat energy.

Try This—Friction Cars

You need: a model car, coarse sandpaper, a table, string, a small plastic pot, and weights

What to do: Tie one end of the string to the front of the model car. Attach the other end to the plastic pot, which should hang down over the side of the table. How much weight do you need to put in the pot to get the car moving? Put sandpaper under the car. Do you need to add more weight to the pot to move the car now? Does this mean that the sandpaper causes a greater friction force than the table?

GRAVITY

Another of Isaac Newton's great achievements was to realize that the force that keeps the moon in **orbit** around the earth is the same force that makes an apple fall to the ground—**gravity**.

Attractive Objects

Every object pulls every other object toward it through the force of gravity. Two cups sitting side by side on a table are attracting each other. But the tiny force they produce is overwhelmed by the massive force of attraction produced by the earth that pulls them down onto the table. The size of the force of gravity depends on two things: the **mass** (the amount of matter it contains) of each object and the distance between them.

Flight Paths and Orbits

The force of gravity pulls all objects equally. This means that two objects dropped at the same time from the same height will reach the ground at the same time. It does not matter whether one is heavier than the other, nor does it matter if one is also traveling forward. A bullet fired from a gun on a level flight path will hit the ground at the same time as one that is simply dropped. Of course, it will fall a lot farther away!

Alan Shepard takes off on his historic flight to the edge of space.

It's a Fact—Into Orbit

The first U.S. astronaut, Alan Shepard, did not make it into orbit because his Redstone Rocket was not powerful enough. He reached a height of 115 miles (185 kilometers) before gravity brought him back down to Earth.

If a bullet, or any other object, travels fast enough, the curve of its path will exactly follow the curve of the earth. It continues to fall, but the surface of the earth is falling away beneath it at the same rate. Instead of hitting the ground, it continues on around the earth. It has gone into orbit.

Center of Gravity

The **center of gravity**, or center of balance, of an object is the point where a single applied force could support it. It is the point where the mass of the object is equally balanced. Objects with a high center of gravity, such as the average person, are unstable. If you lean too far back or to the side, you will begin to fall as gravity pulls you off balance.

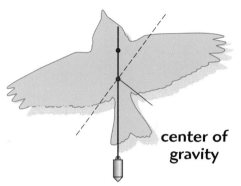

plumb line

Suspend object and plumb line – draw line where plumb line falls

center of gravity

Suspend object from another point and draw line where plumb line falls again – center of gravity is where the two lines cross

Use a plumb line to find the center of gravity.

Try This—Balancing Act

You need: a cork, a needle, two forks, and a piece of string tied between two chair backs

What to do: Push the needle into the bottom of the cork. Then push forks into opposite sides of the cork. Now try to balance the cork on the string on the point of the needle. It should be easier than you think. The heavy forks mean that the center of gravity of your balancer is actually somewhere outside it, directly under the needle. This gives it stability.

WEIGHTS AND MEASURES

There are three ways to change the weight of an object. You can take some of it away so it has less **mass** and therefore becomes lighter. You can add mass to it so it becomes heavier. Or you can make it lighter by taking it into space.

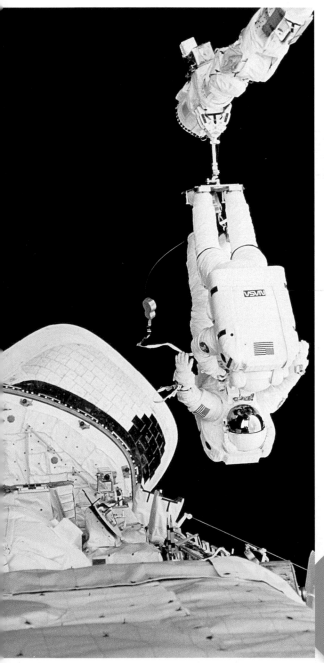

Weight and Gravity

The weight of an object tells you how much the earth's force of **gravity** is pulling on it. An object close to the earth's surface weighs more than one that is far away from it. If you take your object to the moon, which is smaller than the earth and exerts less of a pull, it will weigh less. If you could take it to Jupiter, the biggest of the planets, Jupiter's powerful gravity would make it heavier.

Free Falling

A spacecraft in **orbit** is constantly falling towards the earth without being slowed down by air resistance. As a result, astronauts do not feel the

In the near weightlessness of space, astronauts can move objects that would be impossibly heavy to shift on Earth.

acceleration of gravity, but feel weightless instead. The orbiting astronauts and their spacecraft are not actually weightless. The earth's gravity is still there, but it is not felt as long as the spacecraft is in **free fall**. Space scientists tend to use the term **microgravity** to describe the forces inside a spacecraft—all the objects inside it are attracted to one another.

Newtons

Forces are generally measured in units called newtons. A force of about ten newtons is needed to move a mass of 2.2 lbs (1kg) on the earth. One newton is about the force you would need to lift an apple 3 feet (about a meter) off the ground against the earth's gravity. A typical jet engine exerts a force of about 100,000 newtons.

An astronaut would be three times lighter on Mars than on Earth because of Mars's weaker gravity.

It's a Fact—Weight Changes

If it were possible to stand on Jupiter, you would weigh nearly three times what you do on Earth. On Mars, you would have around a third of your Earth weight.

Try This—Instant Weight Loss!

You need: a bathroom scale

What to do: Stand on the scale. Hold your hands up at shoulder height. Thrust them down quickly. Watch the indicator on the scale go down slightly. Your downward **thrust** is matched by an upward thrust (Newton's third law) that works against gravity, making you momentarily lighter.

TURNING AND SPINNING

If you apply a force to an object that is fixed in one place, but which can turn freely, the object will rotate around the fixed point. This fixed point is called a pivot, or **fulcrum**.

A hammer thrower turns and spins, producing a centripetal force. When she releases the hammer, the centripetal force is removed and the hammer flies off in a straight line.

Turning Forces

The turning effect of a force depends on the **magnitude** of the force and the distance it is applied from the fulcrum. The farther away from the fulcrum the force is applied, the greater the effect will be. Try closing a door by pushing it near the hinges, the door's fulcrum. It is much easier to push when you push near the edge of the door where the handle is.

Going Around in Circles

The propeller on an airplane, the wheels on your bicycle, a CD playing in a stereo system, are all spinning in circles. How is it possible to get continuous circular motion from straight line forces? Spinning objects are changing direction all the time. A turning force, like the one applied to the pedals of a bicycle, sets the wheel in motion. A second force, called the **centripetal force**, pulls the wheel in towards its center, pulling the wheel around and changing its direction continually so it turns in a circle.

Going for a Spin

A **gyroscope** is a kind of spinning top that consists of a wheel and an axle mounted in a frame. When the wheel is spinning rapidly, it has **inertia**, just as any other moving object does. It will resist attempts to change its direction of movement. The axle of a spinning gyroscope always points in the same direction, no matter how the object on which it is standing is moved. Gyroscopes are used to help keep rockets and aircraft on a straight course.

Precession is a special force that makes a gyroscope tend to move at right angles to any force that pushes on it. If you press slowly and steadily on the axle of a spinning gyroscope, it will move to the right or the left, not in the direction in which you are pushing it.

It's a Fact—Gyroscopes in Space

Spacecraft rely on gyroscopes to keep them on course. Magnetic compasses are of no use in space, where there is no Pole for them to point to.

A spinning gyroscope has a great deal of inertia and is difficult to unbalance.

Try This—Pedaling Precession

You need: a bicycle

What to do: You can experience precession for yourself. Lean to one side while you are riding your bicycle, and it will turn that way, even if you keep the handlebars pointing straight ahead.

25

FLOATING AND SINKING

Many things will float on water, from a huge oil tanker to a leaf on a pond. They float because they are being supported by the water.

Buoyancy

The upward push of a fluid on an object is called **buoyancy**. It is not just objects that float that are affected by buoyancy. In the bath or pool, try lifting a leg out of the water. Do you notice that it feels lighter in the water? This is because the water is supporting part of your leg's weight.

Oil is less dense than water and will float on it. This leads to terrible pollution of coasts when tankers run aground.

Sink or Float?

What determines whether an object will sink or float? It is not weight. A whole tree trunk will float just as well as a twig, but even a small pebble will sink. What determines whether or not an object will sink is **density**.

Density measures the amount of material in a given **volume**, calculated by the formula $D = m/V$, where D = density, m = **mass**, and V = volume. Find a rock and a piece of wood of about the same weight.

The weight of the rock is concentrated into a much smaller space than the weight of the wood. The rock is denser than the wood. Fluids also have density. When an object is placed in a fluid, some of the fluid is pushed aside, or displaced. If the fluid is denser than the object, it means that the object weighs less than the fluid it displaces, and the object will float. However, if the fluid is less dense than the object, the object weighs more than the fluid it displaces, and it sinks. Drop the rock and the piece of wood into water. The rock sinks, but the wood floats.

It's a Fact—Dive, Dive, Dive!

A submarine has special ballast tanks inside that are flooded with water when it dives. This increases the submarine's density and causes it to sink. For the submarine to come to the surface again, the water is pumped out of the tanks. Then the submarine rises up through the water again.

Try This—Different Densities

You need: a tall glass, a spoon, syrup, water, and cooking oil

What to do: Carefully pour syrup into the glass. Pour it over a spoon so that it does not get onto the sides of the glass. Next, add some water and finally, some oil, pouring each slowly and carefully over a spoon. The liquids separate into three layers because they each have different densities. You might want to collect a few small objects, such as a cork, a plastic block, a piece of wood, and a piece of pottery, and place them in the jar. Which objects float on which layers?

PRESSURE

What happens when you blow up a balloon? Why should you wear a bicycle helmet? The answers to both questions have to do with **pressure**.

Distributing Forces

What is pressure? To a scientist, it is the force acting on a unit of area of a surface. This is not as difficult as it sounds! A force acting over a small area produces a greater pressure than the same force acting over a large area.

If you wear a bicycle helmet, the force of a collision is spread out over a greater area, helping to protect you from serious injury.

Try pushing your finger into a bulletin board. Then try pushing a thumbtack into the board. The tack goes in easily even though you have probably used more or less the same force. The point of the tack has a far smaller surface area than the tip of your finger. The pressure from the tack is therefore much greater because the force you exert is concentrated into a small area.

Blowing up a balloon makes the air pressure inside it greater than the pressure outside it.

Air Pressure

When you blow up a balloon, the **molecules** of air in the balloon move around very rapidly. The inside of the balloon is being struck by these particles all the time. Every time a particle hits the inside of the balloon, it pushes it out. Molecules in the air hit the outside of the balloon all the time too, pushing it in. All of these tiny impacts added together are what produce air pressure. If the pressure pushing out is greater than the pressure pushing in, the balloon will expand.

A camel's big feet spread the weight of its body over a large area and stop it sinking into the sand.

It's a Fact—Under Pressure

The air in the **atmosphere** around us is so dense that the total air pressure on your body probably amounts to thousands of pounds. The reason you are not aware of this huge force is because the fluid and air in your body pushes out with an equal pressure, balancing the air pressure.

Try This—Water Pressure

Ask an adult to help you with this activity.

You need: a large plastic drink bottle, a basin, a nail, water, and sticky tape

What to do: Puncture a row of three or four holes from top to bottom in the bottle using the nail. Put a strip of tape over the holes to cover them while you fill the bottle with water. Stand the bottle in the basin while you fill it. Now quickly pull the tape off. From which hole does the water squirt farthest? It will go farthest from the lowest hole because of the pressure of water above it forcing it out.

GLOSSARY

acceleration   rate at which **velocity** changes

atmosphere   layer of gases that surrounds the earth

atom   one of the tiny particles of which all materials are made

buoyancy   lifting effect of a fluid on an object that is placed in it

center of gravity   point in or near an object where the effect of gravity on the object is concentrated

centripetal force   inward pulling force that acts on an object moving in a curved path

compress   make more compact by pressing

density   measure of the amount of mass contained within a unit of volume of a particular substance

drag   force that slows down an object as it travels through a liquid or a gas

elasticity   ability of a material to return to its previous shape after being stretched

elastic limit   point at which any further stretching of an object results in it being unable to return to its original shape

elastic potential energy   energy stored in a stretched object that is released when it returns to its original shape

electrostatic   relating to objects that are electrically charged

energy   capacity for doing work

free fall   falling motion of an object that is being attracted by gravity, without being slowed down by air resistance

friction   force that acts to slow down or stop objects that are moving against each other

fulcrum   point or support around which something turns

gravity   force of attraction between objects

gyroscope   fast-spinning wheel; its axis continues pointing in the same direction once the wheel starts spinning

inertia   tendency of an object to remain at rest, or to keep moving in a straight line, until it is acted upon by a force

kinetic energy   energy of a moving object

law   in science, a rule that tells what will happen in a particular set of circumstances. For example, the law of gravity tells how an object acts when acted upon by a gravitational force

lift   upward force that keeps a flying object, such as an aircraft or a bird, in the air

magnetism   force of attraction or repulsion between some materials, such as iron

magnitude   measure of the size of a force

mass   amount of matter, or material, within an object

microgravity   small gravitational forces between objects that are outside the force of gravity of a large object, such as a planet

molecule   two or more atoms joined together

momentum   tendency of a moving object to keep on moving until it is stopped by a force acting on it

orbit   path an object follows as it travels around a larger object

precession   force that tends to make a spinning object move at right angles to a pushing force acting on it

pressure   amount of force pushing on a given area

resultant   force that results when two or more forces are acting on an object

strain   measure of the extent to which an object changes shape when a stress is applied to it

stress   force that acts on an object to change its shape

terminal velocity   velocity a falling object reaches when **acceleration** due to gravity and slowing down due to air resistance balance each other

thrust   propelling force generated by a rocket or an aircraft engine

velocity   measure of speed in a particular direction

volume   space that is taken up by an amount of matter

More Books to Read

De Pinna, Simon. *Forces & Motion.* Chatham, NJ: Raintree Steck-Vaughn. 1998.

Dixon, Malcolm and Karen Smith. *Forces & Movement.* Mankato, MN: Smart Apple Media. 1998.

Gardner, Robert. *Experiments with Motion.* Springfield, NJ: Enslow Publishers. 1995.

Hewitt, Sally. *Forces Around Us.* Danbury, CT: Children's Press. 1998.

Hewitt, Sally. *Full of Energy.* Danbury, CT: Children's Press. 1998.

Marshall, John. *Go & Stop.* Vero Beach, FL: Rourke Book Company. 1995.

Marshall, John. *Motion & Speed.* Vero Beach, FL: Rourke Book Company, 1995.

Taylor, Barbara. *Weight & Balance.* Danbury, CT: Franklin Watts. 1990.

Wheeler, Jill C. *Move It! A Book about Motion.* Minneapolis, MN: ABDO Publishing. 1998.

Wheeler, Jill C. *The Forces with Us: A Book about Energy.* Minneapolis, MN: ABDO Publishing. 1998.

White, Larry. *Gravity: Simple Experiments for Young Scientists.* Brookfield, CT: Millbrook Press. 1995.

Index